A JOURNEY IN THE SPIRIT

This Is My Story, This Is My Song

REVISED EDITION

A JOURNEY IN THE SPIRIT

This Is My Story, This Is My Song

REVISED EDITION

Jessica L. Lucas

New Living Translation Bible scripture quotations reprinted with permission.

King James Version is in the public domain and copyright permission is not required.

David McCasland, Our Daily Bread, Copyright© 2006 by RBC Ministries, Grand Rapids, MI. Reprinted by permission.

This book or parts thereof may not be reproduced by any means in any form without written permission from the publisher — including electronic, mechanical, photocopy and retrieval systems. In addition, reviewers may quote brief passages for a review without prior permission from the publisher.

All rights reserved.

Copyright© 2020 by Jessica Lucas

ISBN: #978-0-578-74767-5

Library of Congress Control Number: 2020918163

This book is dedicated in remembrance of my father, Charles W. Phillips who transitioned on January 31, 2020. Thank you for always believing in me and teaching me to live in the true essence of our Lord. I will always and forever love you.

~Jessica~

Contacting the Author

Jessica Lucas
P.O. Box 6234
Gainesville, FL 32627

E-mail: afreshjourney@gmail.com

Visit

Website: www.jessicallucas.com

Acknowledgements

I would first like to thank my father, the late Charles Wayne Phillips and my mother Janice Phillips for their encouragement and spiritual guidance. To my grandparents, Bishop Emeritus James McKnight, Sr. and Mother Jessie McKnight, for your unwavering faith in the power of prayer, to you I say thank you. To the late Elder Willie Leroy and Mother Willie Lou Phillips, your presence in my life will always be cherished. To my brother Chase Phillips, you have always seemed to make me laugh in even the most trying of times. Thank you for keeping a smile on my face. Finally, to my husband Alonzo, I honor you for your support during this process and truly appreciate you for our partnership.

To Avery McKnight, I never thought this publication would ever come to pass. I thank you for calling forth the writer in me. To my uncle, John McKnight, Sr., I can always count on you for sound wisdom and advice when doubt and uncertainty arise. Thank you; and know that healing is near. To Mr. Michael Foley at the University of Florida's College of Journalism, thank you for pushing me to be the best journalist I can be. To all of my aunts, uncles, cousins, extended family members and friends, thank you for teaching me what it truly means to follow after God's heart when all seems lost

Lastly, I thank all of the youth who contributed their ideas and comments for this publication to bring reality to the Holy Spirit's power on our generation.

Introduction

I pray the Lord's Spirit will flourish as you continue to read the following pages. My aim is that the word of God through my story will become clear and tangible as you search the provided scriptures. Some of you may not have had a true, spiritual encounter with the Holy Spirit, but upon the conclusion of my story I'm certain you will fully know who God is.

The prompting for this autobiography rests solely on the Holy Spirit in His exquisite and unique leading. My ultimate goal is that as you read my personal testimony, you will uncover the glorious ways and manners of our Lord. I pray you will be able to find the strength and deliverance that is ever so applicable to our journey with Christ as you learn of my journey with the King of all Kings. He is the source of holiness, the breath and essence of life sealing our new and renewed relationship with Jesus.

Known as the Comforter and keeper of all things past, present, and to come, the Spirit of God seeks to confirm the promises of the Father by revealing the very nature and being of His son. I declare all access will be granted as you prepare to read my account of God's remarkable presence in my life. I officially announce a new beginning is about to unfold. So, as you ponder what words the Lord has given me to share, open your heart and mind as I take you on a journey in the Spirit.

Table of Contents

Acknowledgements vii

Introduction ix

Chapter 1: Born Twice 1

Chapter 2: The Sound of Heaven 10

Chapter 3: Invisible, but Evident 22

Chapter 4: Going Through the Fire 26

Chapter 5: When God Speaks… 32

Chapter 6: Continual Praise 42

Chapter 7: Accidents Happen 52

Chapter 8: A New Beginning 59

Chapter 9: On a Quest for Love 64

Chapter 10: Learning to Trust in Him 76

Chapter 11: Renewed Faith 87

CHAPTER 1

Born Twice

"Jesus answered and said unto him. Verily, verily, I say unto thee. Except a man be born again, he cannot see the Kingdom of God." John 3:3 (KJV)

On July 17, 1983, I was born all too early at one pound and 4 ounces. It was several months before my prescribed date of arrival, November 1, 1983. My mother had five miscarriages prior to my birth and I was being fed through my hands and feet. With respect to my sight, 2 and ½ months went by before my parents knew I was able to see on my own. Three days after I was born, mom and dad were told I only had a 10 percent chance of living.

I have a quick question for you. If you had the opportunity to choose which one of the five senses to do without for the rest of your life, which one would you choose?

Would you chose your hearing, your sight, or your sense of touch?

On a scale from one to five, one being perfect sight and five being total blindness, the doctors said my number was a four. Thank God for the subtraction of one. Currently, I suffer from astigmatism and I am near-sighted. I wear glasses, but other than that, I am thankful I am able to see.

Tests of different colors, shapes and symbols were brought before me by medical professionals even though I was too young to decipher what my eyes were seeing at the time. I was fed fluids at the most unpopular of places—my head. Needles were intricately placed around the contours of veins and hair as doctors searched for the right spot. A scar, from the result of a damaged heart, is faintly etched on my back. About an inch-and-a-half in length, it reminds me of the open-heart surgery, performed on my tiny, fragile body.

By Tuesday, November 1, the date I was supposed to be born, I was a big and fat 4 ½ pounds. Thanks to the in-home care assistants who attended to me and mom, I grew to become a small baby and that Thanksgiving was a happy one for my parents and the entire family. The struggles I endured during my premature days will forever stay in my mind as I grow in faith. What God has done for me and my family is nothing short of a miracle.

My second birth, 14 years, 4 months (723 weeks and 5 days later) on November 22, 1997 was much easier. During the first, I fought for my life and the second birth, life was given to me. In the first birth, my name was written on paper. The second birth my name was written in God's Book of Life. The first was necessary. The second was essential.

I can still vividly remember the time of my second birth, another Sunday morning had come, but earlier in the month of September, depression and anxiety overwhelmed me for no reason at all. Spiritually, I knew I was not living as I should. At 14, the Holy Spirit was drawing me closer to Christ, but out of ignorance and disobedience, I shunned the voice of the Lord. To be honest, I was tired of living in fear of not knowing where my final destination was going to be. So, to end the uncertainty, I shakily rose from my pew and walked to the altar with tears in my eyes.

Born and raised in the church, I naively thought I would be "grandfathered" into the faith because my grandmother and grandfather were the leaders at my home church in Gainesville, Florida (Gainesville Church of God By Faith.) Because of their relationship, I believed I had a plot where my mansion in heaven was to be built. My father let me know that I couldn't possibly rely on getting to heaven by my relatives. I had to have my own personal relationship with

Jesus. So on that day, I took his words and accepted Jesus as my personal savior.

I would have to say that both births are of equal importance. Not only because God was the main character in both instances, but that in order to be born again, you first, have to be born. The second birthday celebration calls for no cake, presents or ice cream, just a bunch of angels rejoicing in heaven to see a lost sinner accepting Christ's love in salvation. Wow, what a gift!

Shortly after I got saved, I suffered from depression and anxiety for 3 ½ years. It began my sophomore year in high school and ended my sophomore year in college. Through the entire time, I would often find myself questioning the validity of my salvation. I automatically thought life was to be a lot better with Christ. Ultimately, I found that to be true, but later I learned that accepting Christ does not mean trouble, struggles and wrestling with the cares of this world would cease. Just to look at me, you would have not known that sleepless nights and a change in eating habits overwhelmed me to the point where I lost 10 pounds, and my weight dropped down to a whopping 80 pounds.

At church, I still smiled, danced, spoke in tongues and sang like nobody's business. At school, I still went to class as usual and maintained my "B" average. However, home was different altogether. I moped and slugged around, staying in my bedroom whimpering like a small child crying out to God.

I would on occasion come out of my room only to plop in front of the television watching TBN, the Church Channel and other uplifting stations hoping to hear a word from God for my healing. For those few hours, worship replaced grumbling and thankfulness replaced complaining. As this interesting cycle of depression and worship continued, I realized that my praise was not in vain.

I began to see a glimpse of comfort and restoration after I allowed the Holy Spirit to take control. It was during this time that I broke free from the enemy's stronghold over my life. I think a HALLELUJAH is in order!

As I look back on those years, pain brought a greater anointing. Thank God for wisdom and growth because as a young teenager, I only wanted to please people and the close circle of friends I had accumulated. Pleasing God was not on my agenda. In high school, I was the odd ball, the one nobody really wanted to hang with. If someone wanted me to pray for them or to bring some type of encouragement, my classmates would run to me to go to God on their behalf. The struggle of not having any true friends outside of family puzzled me, but the Lord knew my story was unique and some would not understand.

The book of Ecclesiastes Chapter 3 Verse 1 says *"To everything there is a season, and a time to every purpose under the heaven."* Why not consider your time and your purpose from God's perspective? All of us are here for a reason. Once we acknowledge that and know our purpose for being here, then we can truly live the way God sees us.

With me witnessing thousands of invitations to accept Christ, there are not many instances where young people are taking the stand to live for God. As I got older, I wondered why people would not flock to the Lord, I mean He is in fact the Creator of literally everything, so it was strange when the altar would be empty. To shed some light on this premise, I asked several teenagers to share their thoughts on salvation and why the youth are not committing their lives to Christ. Here are their responses.

One young lady said this: "To be born of the Spirit of God [is] to accept Christ as your personal savior. To be 'born again' does not mean that you have to go through the birthing process as you did when you were first born (in the flesh)—but it means that you are made a new person in God and Christ. The significance of the spiritual birth is to show that we are [again] made new in Christ and that we are a child of God. We are only able to serve God in spirit because God is a spirit. Thus, if we are born in the Spirit, then we can serve God."

Another young man commented on spiritual growth and spiritual birth. To him, being born again means to be "removed from sin. To be separated from the world. It is a part of our worship unto God. Spiritual growth means that you are mature in God and [He will] begin to change you on another level. The only way you can do this is through God's power."

Once a person fully experiences the true power of God, they will never be the same. Everything about the person changes, from their attire, to their character and everything associated with their lives becomes a testament of God's supernatural power. So, why aren't more young people getting saved? "It is all because of fear," says one teenage girl. "It is more peer-pressure [than they can handle]. They think about what people are going to say and they become fearful and afraid. Or, they get saved one time and they do the same sinful things over and over. They have betrayed their commitment to God by doing so." Again, fear is the main factor, says another teen.

"They fear that people will look at them [if they consider salvation]. It scares them off from being baptized in the Holy Ghost. They also fear change in their lifestyle. There is always an excuse. They don't think the Word of God pertains to them. Either they blame church or church leaders for their reluctance in salvation."

If you are reading this and have not experienced the free gift of salvation, I admonish you to search the scriptures and find what it takes for you to save yourself from eternal destruction. Romans 10:9, Romans 13:11, 2 Corinthians 6:2, Mark 16:16, John 3:17, Acts 16:31, and Philippians 2:12 are all great places to start. Pray and seek the Lord while He may be found. Search for Him with all of your heart in sincerity. Continue to stay strong in the faith and I hope to see you one day in glory.

The rest and joy of the Lord redeems all sorts of confusion by signifying His role as the second Adam. No matter what your personal beliefs are concerning the sin of Adam and Eve, we were all born into sin for God blew the law of creativity into Adam, not Eve. When he ate the forbidden fruit, Adam's mistake resulted in us being at fault. This is why Christ (the second Adam) had to become the first Adam (of creation) to rectify what occurred in Genesis Chapter 3.

Like Christ, we are to be an exact reflection of Him. In the natural, our mothers and fathers define who we are until we are old enough to come into our own. In the Spirit, you are marked for life. Just when you were born and had some form of a "birth mark" to confirm your existence, there is a spiritual "birth mark" confirming your relationship with the Father. The moment you said "Yes," you were within nanoseconds of freely receiving every spiritual gift imaginable and opened the opportunity of eternal life from the start.

All things will become secondary once we take on the mind of Christ.

Trusting in your own mindset will only lead to destruction, for the ways that seem right unto men, the end thereof is destruction. But, when we set our mind and our affections on Christ, He will give us all that is true, right and holy. Stop doing what you have been accustomed to, if you want the unmerited favor of God. Go outside of the box in your service to the Lord and watch how He responds. If you want something you've never had, then you have to do something you've never done. There has to be a change in the amount of time spent in prayer with God. A change in your worship has to take place as well as a change in your submission. It's all up to you whether you are going to do it now or later.

CHAPTER 2

The Sound of Heaven

"And they were all filled with the Holy Ghost and began to speak with other tongues as the Spirit gave them utterance." Acts 2:4 (KJV)

It's time to go to the forefront with a sound. What do you sound like? In respect to my life, even before I was able to speak in clear sentences as a young child, I was taught to sing in every facet of the ministry by the age of 2. I owe it all to a young lady talented in the arts of theater, song and creativity. It is to her I give my gratitude and thanks for birthing songs in my heart that are still being sung today.

I and several other youngsters in the mid 80s and early 90s were a part of countless talent shows, musicals, skits, plays (in church as well as the community) and other events showcasing our talents and gifts that were only opened and complete through God. Singing taught me how to bring words to life from my inner man that couldn't otherwise be spoken or written. Ephesians 5:19 sums up what I felt as a young girl singing unto the Lord.

"Speaking to yourselves in psalms and hymns and spiritual songs, singing and making melody in your heart to the Lord."

When I sing, I am literally transported into the presence of God—every time, even outside of the church walls. Whenever a song pops up, with eyes closed and a heart filled with joy, the scene changes to a large spiritual music box where tunes are played on cue. In developing my own language with the Lord while trying to deal with moments of suicidal thoughts and trying to nail this whole "saved" thing, I was longing and yearning for something more.

I wanted God—the Holy Spirit to come down from His space in heaven to visit me in such a way that I knew I was changed for the better. I wanted lights, I wanted smoke and I wanted thunder. I wanted to hear God's voice along with the glory of the Lord to fill my soul, literally. In some cases, God will move by mighty acts, signs and wonders, but at other times, He will move in secret, quietly and unnoticeable to the spiritually impaired.

The importance of sound and declaring vocally what you specifically want from the Lord moves him to act on your behalf. For some, your breakthrough will not come until you literally open your mouth and speak the promises of God, or just use every fiber in your being to yell, shout, and scream the declarations of God in order to receive your answer. I have done this on numerous occasions and it works. We have to learn to be persistent, conscientious and strategic in the things we are asking of Him. Before I continue, I want to describe the certain level of sound and noise that must be reached to ensure the authentic presence of the Lord. In a sermon taught by a popular bishop seen on television, his analysis on sound derived from several heavenly attributes.

"Sound is the entrance for glory," the bishop said. This means God will operate fully only when a certain level of sound or "praise" is achieved by the believer. Acts Chapter 2, Verse 2 explains this premise. From the King James Version, the Bible says: *"And suddenly there came a sound from heaven as of a rushing mighty wind, and it filled all the house where they were sitting."* In this particular passage, the sound was doing three things, he said. "It was rushing, it was mighty and there was a wind." The pressure or the disturbance from heaven caused such a stir among the 120 individuals, who were anxiously waiting for the opportunity from God to be released in the upper room.

Sound is the identifier, the bishop said, and praise is the signature mark that reveals the workings of God and the Holy Spirit. "Mighty represents fidelity," the pastor declared to the congregation. Fidelity, or the faithfulness from the participants in the upper room making the "sound," can be compared to wind. It comes from the North, South, East and West, he said.

There is no limit to where the sound is coming from because all space, the entire structure of the small upstairs room, was filled to capacity and overflowing with the impartation that could have only come from the source where all is heard—the Holy Ghost. I revealed this information to indicate how sound directly correlates to the functionality of heaven. In response to this message, the following word came to me on July 6, 2006. This is a prophetic and resounding word for the youth to stand as never before.

> *"I've been hearing much lately concerning the youth as a whole in our inability to really understand our place in the Kingdom of God. That's why I think the young people are not seeking the face of God as they should because the spirit of deliverance and breakthrough is foreign to them.*
>
> *Worship to us is just another part of the service and after seeking the Lord at the altar for about 15 to 20 minutes, we don't feel anything because we haven't grasped the real essence of God's power. I guess that's why we are afraid to position ourselves into the different avenues of ministry. We don't realize that He wants to reinstall some programs from the "old"*

> church. Yes, I'm talking about the real, pure, unaltered, unadulterated power of the Holy Spirit. That is the thing missing from the youth in their spiritual walk."
>
> That's the thing that kept our parents and our grandparents. That's why deliverance, salvation, the filling and re-filling of the Holy Ghost, the gifts and works of the Spirit were so easily obtainable back then. They understood the ways and mannerisms of the Holy Ghost."

I became bi-lingual during my sophomore year at Eastside High School in the fall of 1998. It was a hot night in September. The air was filled with chirping and singing from crickets and fireflies illuminating the sweaty evening in the country. For me, it was an evening filled with geometry problems, postulates, isosceles triangles, measurements, graphing paper, protractors and angles of all sorts.

The time was 11:10 p.m. and my homework assignment was due in two days. Yes, I do agree that having a textbook open with papers sprawled around a bed at that time is silly, but not uncommon to exceptional students. I was getting tired and was about to fall asleep when the Holy Spirit instructed me to turn on the television. I fought the sleepiness to struggle to find the remote. The TBN Channel had the

"This Is Your Day" broadcast on hosted by a prominent pastor in the healing ministry, who was often seen wearing a white suit and a colorful tie. I'll never forget the point that brought me to tears in God's presence as I felt liked I slipped into God's heavenly bedroom. The image still stands vividly in my mind as I saw a young man on the television program with a green T-shirt, blue jeans and white sneakers. He was in the final stages of the HIV/AIDS virus. A mass of skin and bones with spots dotting his body, the pastor pointed in his direction and he fell to the platform under the power of God. When he got up from the floor, it seemed that his skin began to get clearer right before my eyes. I began to instantly praise the Lord for what I had seen and I eventually got lost in my worship. Prior to that miracle, I had never seen anything of that magnitude. After the program, this pastor normally prays for people to be healed from various sicknesses and diseases and would sometimes have a Word of Knowledge about several things. This particular evening he said: "There is a young lady who's in the presence of God right now and in the next few moments, you are going to start praying in tongues." Carnally, I thought he was speaking about someone else, but in a few seconds my mouth opened and unfamiliar words and syllables began to come forth.

I didn't even ask for this gift, but at age 15, I knew I had another outlet to reach the heavenlies. What I thought was to last a few seconds actually lasted 45 minutes. I didn't have to enroll in a class to teach me how to pray in the Holy Ghost. All I had to do was turn on the television. The power of God through my prayer language spewed from my mouth at that precise instant.

Some things in life call for an extra boost in prayer. Sometimes your deliverance will only come from praying in the Spirit. It's a way to get God's attention, a sort of direct line of communication. In recent years and even now, there has been a lot of controversy surrounding whether or not speaking in tongues constitutes someone being filled with the Holy Spirit.

First, in order to pray in the Spirit, you must be filled with the Spirit. You can't pray in something unless that something is fully functioning in you. Second, love must be the recurring foundation for all things spiritual as well as natural. Without love, there would be no need for tongues, prophecy or good deeds as 1st Corinthians Chapter 13 says. Your tongue-speaking prophesying self will be in vain without Christ's greatest commandment.

What occurred in the upper room was stupendous nonetheless in the book of Acts, but the difference is they were not merely voicing sounds; their "tongues" were foreign dialects of those in attendance who gathered from various parts of the world. So, in short, someone understood what those early Christians were saying even though we need some form of interpretation. For those who are new to this experience, don't concern yourself with how you sound because you are not praying from your mouth, you are praying from your heart.

The Word of God offers several scriptures on the importance of praying in the Holy Ghost. "Praying in the Holy Ghost is praying according to the will of God," says a seasoned prayer warrior. "The will of God is the Word of God." The scripture says in Romans 8:26, *"Likewise the Spirit also helpeth our infirmities for we know not what we should pray for as we ought: but the Spirit itself maketh intercession for us with groanings which cannot be uttered."*

Jude 20 reads, *"But ye beloved, building up yourselves on your most holy faith, praying in the Holy Ghost."* So, then how is our faith measured, or better yet, how do we know we are using faith? The scripture in Romans 10:17 states *"So then faith cometh by hearing, and hearing by the Word of God."*

Another factor in praying in the Holy Ghost is abiding by the Word of God. *"If ye abide in me, and my words abide in you, ye shall ask what ye will, and it shall be done unto you." (John 15:7).* Praying in the Spirit will also accurately and completely answer your prayers. Yes, I agree that praying in the natural is best at times, but for those times when you don't know what to pray for, transition to your heavenly tongue.

I may not understand what I'm saying, which is fine because half the time I don't know what I'm saying in English much less the Spirit. All I know is, there is power—much power when I begin to pray in my heavenly prayer language.

Peter understood perfectly what was going on. The prophet Joel was on point when he prophesied that God was going to pour out His Spirit on all flesh. He declared that your sons and daughters shall prophesy, old men will be dreaming and young men will see visions. Even the servants and the handmaids that cater to their masters will feel the weight of His glory. (Joel 2:28-29).

What they saw and experienced was the promise of the Father to His children not to leave them comfortless. Isn't it good to know that God keeps His word? If you'd like to receive the Holy Ghost, there are several practical ways to receive. 1. Ask a Holy Ghost-filled minister of the gospel to lay hands on you, so they can speak the word of the Lord with boldness and confidence. *"And when Paul Had laid hands upon them, the Holy Ghost came on them; and they spake with tongues, and prophesied" (Acts 19:6).* 2. Simply pray and ask God for it. The Holy Spirit will allow shyness and laziness to cease while accepting acts of boldness and clarity. *"And when they had prayed, the place was shaken where they were assembled together; and they were all filled with the Holy Ghost, and they spake the Word of God with boldness" (Acts 4:31).*

I've learned during prayer time to be specific.

Let God know exactly what you want so you won't be surprised when God answers you with an undesirable reply of "No" or "Wait". He might give you your "Yes." It all depends on His will for your life.

The power of the floor is another position in prayer that will literally push you to the threshold of His throne room without any gatekeepers to instruct the proceeding of your entrance. The mere act of lying prostrate on the floor grants your access to His living quarters. This position of prayer will likely warrant much silence and sometimes God will force you to wait in His presence before He will answer your prayers.

Sometimes just lying still is all you need for your breakthrough. No movement or any major action on your part. Just allowing yourself to be broken before the Lord might just cause something magnificent to happen.

The waiting period can be burdensome at times when weeks, months and years go by without closure, but remember God is operating in a different time frame. One-thousand years are as one day the Bible says, so don't give the Lord a deadline to when He should give you a response. While in the waiting room, worship and thanksgiving should occupy your time while delving into God's word for strength, comfort and solace.

Clearing your body from all unrighteousness is perfect for His glory to shine through you and change your situation. Zechariah 2 and 13 says *"Be silent, O all flesh, before the Lord: for he is raised up out of his holy habitation. "*

Holiness also brings silence when lifestyles are in evaluation or when the earth itself is going through transition with various weather conditions, plagues, disasters and devastating destruction. Habakkuk 2: 20 states *"But the Lord is in his holy temple, let all the earth keep silence before him."* It may seem as if God has turned His face, but it is a test to see if you and the body of Christ will graduate to the next dimension of faith, love and commitment in serving as a son or daughter of God.

In our silence, we are sometimes confused about what form of praying God desires. We ask the Lord to teach us how to pray, but He has already given a lesson on how we should pray with the model from the Lord's Prayer in Matthew Chapter 6. By praying and interceding in the Spirit, we experience a transformation in our spiritual growth into the maturity of being conformed to the image and likeness of Jesus. The silence we receive from God will cause us to appreciate His response.

In this time, as I said, we often feel lonely and forgotten, likes God has abandoned us in our greatest time of need. We fail to realize that God was there all the time. He never left, but it is up to us to pursue Him. In our pursuit, praying in the Spirit allows us to enjoy the mercies and promises of God declared in His Word.

CHAPTER 3

Invisible, but Evident

"For the invisible things of him from the creation of the world are clearly seen, being understood by the things that are made, even his eternal power and Godhead; so that they are without excuse."
Romans 1:20 (KJV)

During my senior year in high school, I was dating a young man. He was tall, smart and a good basketball player. He attended many church services and even sang in the choir at times, but the downfall was that he was not saved and I was determined that while we were together, he would confess his salvation.

Seven months of pep rallies, basketball games, youth revivals, band performances and church services occupied most of my time while we were dating. Once he revealed to me that he was not saved, I should have ended the relationship right then and there, but I didn't. I knew that spiritually, the relationship would not work because we were unequally yoked. I had, better yet we had created an illegal soul tie that could only be untied by the Holy Spirit.

He was 6 foot 3, good looking, charming and an awesome athlete with a promising future. But with all of those qualities, he was not the one for me, for the Bible says in 2 Corinthians 6:14 we should *"not be yoked together with unbelievers. For what do righteousness and wickedness have in common? Or what fellowship can light have with darkness?"* *(NIV)* He knew where I stood with my faith, but we both knew that what we tried to create would be short-lived. We ended our relationship one month before my senior prom.

We kept in contact after I graduated from high school. Fortunately, he knew that he had to develop a relationship with the Lord if he was to ever be with me again. About a year after our break up, he called to see how I was doing. I knew that this would be the perfect opportunity to witness to him the love and the forgiveness of the Lord, even though he was very familiar with the gospel message. After our conversation, I became really adamant with him about giving his life to the Lord, for real this time! I wanted him to understand the seriousness of his salvation. He thanked me for my concern and promised to "have a little talk with Jesus" later that evening. A few days later, I got a phone call from his brother saying that he did get saved. My response, "For real, WOW! I could get used to this witnessing thing."

After the phone call, I never felt so happy for someone else finding Christ. The whole weekend I praised God for my friend coming to the Lord. I also discovered that God could speak in and through me. I didn't have to be behind a pulpit with a microphone, a book full of notes and a highlighted Bible to deliver the gospel.

The Spirit of the Lord is kind, gentle and inviting. I like to refer to the Holy Spirit as filtered water without anything artificial or any chemicals. Or, it could be compared to honey from the beehive, not the pasteurized substance from the jar. The Holy Spirit is an inspiration to writers, such as me, journalists, painters, carpenters, musicians, dancers and all other creative minds.

During the initiation of this book, I suffered from writer's block for a couple of days. During that time, I searched for people to give me their comments and opinions on various subjects that I was planning to discuss in the book. Without even knowing it, someone instructed me to consider Philippians 4:13 which says *"I can do all things through Christ which strengtheneth me."*

I glanced at the scripture without one thought. I read it again and the Lord spoke and asked "Who wrote the Bible?" I answered, "Several of your disciples and many other men of God who followed you." He said I was incorrect. He asked me the question again and gave me some time to answer. I said to the Lord that sI didn't know. He said "You should know because He is living in you." Suddenly, it was like a light bulb clicked on in my head. The Holy Spirit, of course was the inspiration for the Bible. One scripture in the book of Job testifies to this statement. *"But there is a spirit in man and the inspiration of the Almighty giveth them understanding." (Job 32:8 KJV)*

The spirit of inspiration broke the silence of my pen and opened my understanding to what God wanted me to say concerning His people through my testimony. Even with reading and re-reading familiar scriptures, it is exciting to anticipate what we will learn from the Holy Spirit as we read the Bible every day. As we leaf through its pages, the Holy Spirit longs to show us something new and refreshing.

CHAPTER 4

Going Through the Fire

"If any man's work shall be burned, he shall suffer loss: but he himself shall be saved; yet so as by fire."
1 Corinthians 3:15 (KJV)

Six months was left until I was to receive my Associate's degree from community college. Thursday, December 12, 2002 I was taking a break from my classes at Santa Fe Community College in Florida, so I decided to check my e-mail messages on my computer.

After a little morning inspiration from several preachers on television and replying to about six e-mails, I heard a muffled flump from behind me. I was thinking *"Oh great, a log shifted in the fireplace. I'll just get the tongs, reposition the log and clean up the mess."* I did just that and vacuumed the hot ashes that fell on the floor. I replaced the vacuum in the closet and everything was back to normal, or so I thought.

I turned around and saw smoke coming from the closet where I placed the vacuum cleaner. I reluctantly walked to the door, opened it and flames engulfed coats,

sweaters and shirts. An inferno of heat filled the closed quarters. I freaked. I didn't know how to operate the fire extinguisher, so after about a minute of my mind blanking out, I called my grandfather and then my father. I also called 9-1-1. Fire trucks were there within 15 minutes. I ran outside the house to my mother as I heard my father's bullets from his gun cabinet flare off. All of his awards and medals as a deputy sheriff were gone in an instant.

Shock slowly crept over me and I assured the firefighter that I was OK. I was hysterical by this point, so to comfort me the firefighter wrapped me in a spotted gray overcoat and gave me a small brown teddy bear that had a baby blue bow tie. As I walked away from my burning home with my parents and my brother, the fire reminded me of two stories that happened in the Old Testament concerning fire. One is in Isaiah Chapter 43 where God promises Jacob and Israel protection. The other story is in Daniel Chapter 3 and involves three Hebrew boys who refused to bow down to a king.

In Isaiah 43:2, the Lord promised *"...when you walk through the fire, you will not be burned; the flames will not set you ablaze." (NIV)* I was able to walk away from the fire without a scratch. My clothes didn't even have a scent of smoke on them. I knew from that moment God's protection was real and happens every day, even when we don't recognize His grace. The New Year in 2003 was spent in an upscale apartment complex on the luxurious side of town, while we waited on our home to be renovated.

I never knew what consecration meant until after about a week's stay during my family's time of displacement at the apartment. The 3-bedroom, 3-bathroom apartment was furnished with a huge walk-in closet. The space in the closet, would have been perfect for hide-and-seek, but served as my temporary prayer room, or rather, a prayer closet. Every evening from 10 to 11, I disposed of sin and re-evaluated my Christian lifestyle through prayer, worship and scripture in that closet.

I remember one night, I began to quietly sing a worship song to set the atmosphere to inviting the presence of the Lord into the closet. Suddenly, I felt the temperature begin to rise. I began to get really hot and subconsciously I knew that it was time to go in major worship mode. What I thought was a few minutes, was actually several hours in prayer. My mouth became dry and all I could say was "Jesus" in a soft whisper. Soon afterwards, I began to sweat and "see" that I was praying in the Spirit. I was confused. Not only by what I was praying in my heavenly tongue in my mind, but I saw a slide-show of what I was praying in the Spirit. My prayer was transformed into a slide-show with pictures showing the tour of heaven as John saw it in Revelation 21 along with significant events in Jesus' ministry, like his baptism in the Jordan River and the miracle at Canaan when he turned water into wine.

The mini-movie forced me to see stories that I had heard as a child. I eventually fell asleep, yes, in the closet, and my movie ended. After my spiritual encounter, the Lord spoke to me and said that He was about to open my eyes and ears to the things of the Spirit. All I could say as a response was "Thank You." After that night in the closet, consecration has become a part of my devotion unto the Lord.

After about 2 months of picking out color combinations for the carpeting, floors, cabinets, tile, bedrooms and countertops, it was time for my family to move back home. Contractors and construction workers were assembled to restore our two-story country home. My father was now able to go back to being the farmer of our small ranch. Many of our mementos and photographs were lost, but our family began anew with the things God spared. From the outside, you would not have known the house had undergone an enormous blow out, but the protective, invisible barrier of the Holy Spirit preserved what He wanted to keep. When we moved back into our home in May of 2003, the furnishings, our lives and our spirits were new.

The other event is in Daniel Chapter 3. What happened to these young men also illustrated God's protection. Nebuchadnezzar was deemed king and he made a golden image, maybe of himself, or one of the many gods that were worshipped, and called for his staff, close attendants, rulers, governors and judges of the land. After gathering everyone together, the Bible tells of an announcer who declared that all should bow and worship the golden image when they heard the music.

For those who did not follow the instructions of worshipping the golden idol, they were to be cast into a fiery furnace. The three Hebrew men refused to obey the declaration and went against the order set by the king. Upon hearing their reason for not bowing, the king was SO furious, he commanded the furnace to be turned up seven times hotter than normal. If I were in that situation, I would seriously consider the urgency of obedience to the king, and to the Holy Spirit before voicing my answer. I would take careful consideration before I said "No."

But as the Hebrews were thrown into the fire, an angel of the Lord intercepted the enemy's plan of destruction. The king was so astonished that he blessed the God of Israel. Nebuchadnezzar therefore made another decree that if anyone spoke evil against the God of Shadrach, Meshach and Abednego, they would be cut into little pieces and their house would be destroyed *"...for no other God can save in this way."* *(Daniel 3:29 NIV)*

Without having been summoned to the king's court, the Hebrew boys were promoted. Every time I think about the fire, without the smell or trace of smoke, I thank God for His unwavering protection in the face of danger. It is very easy to take God's love for granted in our lives and we often forget the little things. His mercy and His grace are new every morning, so in times of life-threatening events, we need to be thankful for the provisions that God gives us.

Maneuvering in life is not always a bowl of tropical fruit and whipped cream. Sometimes life will bring you to a redefining point where God will literally allow the burning of your materials and other collectibles to cause you to organize your lifestyle by adding the Holy Spirit to your daily ritual and routine. The testing and essence of faith must be tried by fire in order to reveal the precious praise and glory of God that will appear as a result of our fellowship with Christ.

CHAPTER 5

When God Speaks...

"In the beginning was the Word, and the Word was with God, and the Word was God."
John 1:1 (KJV)

What are you saying? In your conversation, in your speech, in your actions, in your friendships, in your relationships, in your family, in your workplace and in your leisure time, what is being spoken? There is a familiar saying that says your actions speak louder than your words, but your words have as much power, if not greater than your actions. Promising certain things can become tarnished if you don't follow through or carry out what you promised. As a result, people won't trust you if you continue to not keep promises.

Everything that came out of the mouth of God came to pass, sometimes within seconds even. From the birds of the air and the dolphins of the sea to the rising of Lazarus from his temporary slumber, the Word of God is forever and living. If you are willing to deposit a word daily into a person, then God will have to fill your spirit with His Rhema word to continue establishing the words of life and ministry unto His people.

The Word of God is the definition, explanation and expression of God, according to the Recovery Version Testament. "Hence, it is God defined, explained and expressed." His word is constantly in operation and is always definite, unlike the words of men, which are not always stable and can cause unhappiness and confusion when they cut and shatter a person's feelings. So, if you want God's fullness, speak life to dead situations, speak peace to fits of mayhem and terror, speak love to those individuals that you don't like and most importantly, speak of Jesus to the lost souls of this deteriorating world.

There are countless scriptures dealing with what we say and how we should say it. Our mouthpieces should be an organ of faith, verbalizing the promises and the Word of God, but the enemy will cause us to become mute. He will allow us to become silent when unbelief and doubt are present.

Faith is the only ingredient needed to speak and declare with boldness what the Lord has shown. Faith believes in things that are not in sight, but faith is also senseless and has nothing to do with how you see, taste, smell, feel or hear. Your hunger should be to win lost souls for the kingdom, and not to gain what you can from the world. God did not save you just to be a member of the church and to be selfish with your salvation. God along with heaven rejoices at one lost sinner coming to Christ, not by you attending service every week and worrying only about you and your household. Learn to be a blessing to others by your witness.

We should also be passionate about fulfilling the mission of Jesus in completing the Great Commission found in Matthew 28: 19-20. In order to be in a position of service to the commission of the Lord; we should clear all gateways of our body and spirit of filth and sin. Clean your ears so you can hear God's voice. Open your eyes to allow the sight of the Lord to fill your vision. Clean up your mouth of all unholy speech and conversation.

While trying to clear up the spots in your life, what if God all of a sudden becomes silent? Who will speak to you then? Who will provide you words of encouragement or comfort? I was responding to an e-mail from a friend around midnight one night. My friend and I were planning to begin consecrating ourselves for a period of time. When the day arrived, the first night was an awesome evening of prayer and fasting, but something felt oddly strange a few hours after our devotion.

We both felt for some reason that our lives were not in the will of God anymore and that what we proclaimed in our salvation was a lie from what we were actually representing. In just a few short hours, the enemy had us both brainwashed into believing that we were failures unto the Lord and our bodies and spirits were numb to the grip of the adversary. Discouragement had set in and we felt devastated like the Lord had left us out to dry when we were trying to do something for Him.

In response to my friend in letting him know how I felt, the question came to my mind. What if God is silent? I e-mailed him what the Lord had given me to speak to our situation.

What will we do when the music stops, the band goes home, the shouting is over, the floor is clear and the preacher has gone to his car? After the benediction, then what happens next?

When God begins to truly speak to you, the silence will break. Let Him cheerfully and freely speak in and through you when the time arises. And always remember to follow the instructions He gives you in obedience without grudging or without any trouble. It is so much easier to do what He tells you the first time because you will save time, tears, heartache and difficulty.

You say, "How will I recognize His voice? How will I know it's not my voice or the devil's voice?" Let me help you out a little. The enemy will never encourage you to go forth in the Lord. Any time the Word comes out, there is a significant purpose and meaning for your life, but the tactics of the enemy are to deter the plans of God. You will usually question the leading of the Lord because in most cases you will somehow find a way to back out of what you think God has said. I'm not speaking of all individuals because there are some who instantly know when God is voicing His thoughts and His heart. Sheep recognize their master's voice, but when you are a lamb, you have to be trained to follow your leader.

In my relationship with the Lord, I have found that He will speak to me in the dead of night. Yes, it's a struggle to wake from slumber at 3 and 4 in the morning, An intercessor should pray and learn the mysteries of the Lord. The devil is extremely busy taunting and leading people astray during these hours, and God's special prayer warriors should be on the watch in prayer covering His people during that time.

When I wake in the early morning, I will often write what He has said on a note pad so I won't forget or miss what He has told me. Sometimes, you may not know the vision or the dream in its totality because He does not reveal everything to you all at once for you might become overwhelmed. God usually reveals visions in parts so the transition to the completion of the vision will be more practical.

In late April of 2006, I had the privilege to travel to Los Angeles, California to attend the 100 year Celebration of Azusa where the outpouring of the Holy Spirit fell in 1906. The Kodak and Chinese Theatres, the Hollywood Walk of Fame and the ever-popular Rodeo Drive were only some of the attractions that piqued my interest.

Yes, the shopping was expensive, but the reason I flew for 5 hours was to be part of the Holy Spirit experience. So, when my 3 roommates from New York wanted to go to the Chinese Theatre to hopefully see some celebrities, I had to decline. I wanted to spend time with God. Wow, that's not normal for a 22-year-old who was in one of the most attractive cities in the U.S. From the first day I arrived, I was surrounded by family and friends who dragged me to retail shops, restaurants and malls to get the entire Los Angeles experience.

The facilitators, choirs, concerts and special guests were enlightening, but it was not until Wednesday evening of the conference, which was April 26, that I had the opportunity to be alone. I did not immediately go to God in prayer. Before I settled myself with the Holy Spirit, I decided to watch some television first. So I sat on the bed surfing the television for a Lifetime movie. I had already seen the movie that was airing before, so I turned the television off. I got up and walked to the refrigerator that was oddly placed under a counter full of curling irons, lotion, hair spray, combs and perfume. I knelt and found the half empty bottle of my Minute Maid orange juice.

As I returned to the bed to get some sleep, it was still early, 9:45 p.m. to be exact. I could not go to sleep. I needed something to do and I regretted not going with the girls to Hollywood. The Lord answered my dilemma. *"I had to get you by yourself so you could feel me again."* He instructed me to clean up the room, so I decided to call housekeeping for a special cleaning and He said *"No, I want you to clean it."* I was astonished and said *"Lord, I am paying your people, your daughters of cleanliness to assist in what you have called them to do."* I thought his next answer was hilarious. *"You think you are so smart because you are in college? Well, then begin to rearrange the dominion of comfort."*

After that I began to fold the clothes we had worn the previous day and put them in the plastic bags. I made the beds, cleaned the counters and desks and organized the food in the refrigerator. I said, *"OK Lord, now what?"*

God responded, *"Now that you have completed the task of cleaning the room, I want you to kneel and say my name until you can't do so anymore."*

I thought, *"Here it is! I am about to go somewhere beautiful."*

I began to call on the name of Jesus like the saints used to do in the old church. I stopped after I felt a rumble in my stomach. Maybe I needed to eat something, I thought, to satisfy the hunger. God said that I did, but not physically. The warm sensation around my stomach area became stronger every time I said "Jesus." I knew there was power in His name, but I had no idea the magnitude of how great His name actually was. I did not keep track of the time because my friends would often set their clocks for about an hour or so to be considered "super spiritual" in His presence, but they soon learned not to put a time limit on the Lord, so I didn't either. I shook ferociously under the power of God right there on the hotel room floor. What seemed like hours were only a few moments as my cell phone displayed that only 15 minutes had passed. By that time it was 10 p.m.

Isn't it strange that when you are in the earth realm, you can't wait until the clock reaches a certain time to do the things that need be done? When in the Spirit, the reverse happens. You want to stay on the floor or wherever the presence of the Lord appears.

After about an hour and forty-five minutes, yes, to me that is a LONG TIME, I really could not speak anymore and I felt as though I had returned from a heated sauna. I felt heavy and weak, like in travail. Shakily, I rose and walked back to the bed to get some sleep. Now, it was almost midnight and my roommates returned. They knew that something had happened. I was hoarse, but I told them I was in prayer. For them, that was it; they knew the power prayer.

My stay in California lasted for one week and I returned to Orlando, Florida. After a few days in celebration of my uncle's pastoral celebration, I finally made it back to the little country settlement of Copeland that Sunday afternoon.

Two months later on Thursday, July 6, I was taking a nap and I dreamt of flames surrounding people dressed in white who were bowing to Jesus, who stood in the center of a bank of water. I heard wails, screams, praise and prayers. I was in the midst of the people and in my dream I heard myself pray these words:

"Pray for the winds of Azusa to sweep and breathe through the body like a rushing storm. The flames of 1906 will rekindle and burn from the days of old so that we may realize the true authority of Pentecost and what REALLY HAPPENED in the Upper Room.

s I want my generation to learn the secrets of tapping into the mysteries of the Holy Spirit by searching the Word of God and by pursuing the majesty of our King. The Holy Ghost says that we need to be ferocious in our intimacy with Him. This is not just something we do on certain days, but we need to know how to stay at His feet for HOURS if need be. Praying in our spiritual language for HOURS, DAYS, WEEKS and MONTHS if necessary, to listen to the voice of the Lord in DAILY INTERCESSION."

As my prayer ended, the people rose and declared holy living by saying:

"We SHALL live Holy. We will renounce the things of this world and live in accordance with God's Word. We are that peculiar people that will be separate by not CONFORMING to this earth realm, but we WILL be OPEN to the things of the Spirit and CONFORM to the works of heaven." Amen!

CHAPTER 6

Continual Praise

"I will bless the Lord at all times; His praise shall continually be in my mouth."
Psalms 34: 1 (KJV)

Hallelujah, thank you, Jesus. We bless Your holy name. Lord, we love You. Statements of this sort rang through the modern-day church for years by praise teams, choirs, musicians, facilitators, and pastors.

My question to you my friend is who is the author of your praise? Do you rely on a group of singers to initiate your thankfulness? Do you only dance when the organ hits that certain note, or will we find you in the parking lot shouting without any musical assistance?

Are you one of those members who has to be asked to lift your hands and say amen? What if the atmosphere is not quite to your liking in the sanctuary, for some reason?

Will you still participate in the worship service, or worse, will you simply leave?

Many of us have asked these questions at some point and you wonder why sometimes church can be boring. The answer is because you did not make it exciting. What does it really mean to "go to church" anyway? Shouldn't the "church" already be a part of us? The act of worship is uplifting and necessary for spiritual success and is dependent on your personal reverence and admiration for God.

Scripture says that not only must we worship in spirit and truth, but that an acceptable form of praise would be to, *"Enter his gates with thanksgiving; go into his courts with praise. Give thanks to him and praise his name"* (Psalms 100:4 NLT). If we are to be doers of the Word, then why is this scripture so difficult for us to obey? Only heaven knows.

I remember how God taught me the importance of continual, perpetual praise through the fiery trial of failure. During my first semester at the University of Florida in August 2003, some of my courses were extremely difficult and I was having a hard time keeping my grades up.

In the end, I lost my scholarship and was put on academic probation. To say the least, I was devastated because up until this point I had maintained a "B" average in my coursework. This experience forced me to remain thankful even though I knew I had to work even harder to regain my scholarly status. The next semester I redeemed myself and received a satisfactory report.

Yes, I took God for granted. In my mind I thought I was supposed to have a prosperous and enjoyable life without any problems. Wow, was I clueless! I never really learned how to praise God or even pray for myself because everything (spiritually speaking) was decided for me.

I had to sing in 2 of the 4 choirs at our church. After all, I was the Bishop's granddaughter. When I served, I would not feel any pleasure because my heart was not in it. Unfortunately, I thought I was doing God a favor. My prayer life was extremely poor and I am sad to say I relied on my family and church family to sustain me spiritually. I was ignorant of what a privilege having a relationship with the Lord is, but all the while I still claimed my salvation was as tight as a magician in a straight jacket.

My first month at a large university with about 50,000 students, along with my hectic schedule brought back symptoms of anxiety and suicidal thoughts. My study habits needed improvement. I was struggling with my courses and I regretted being on campus. I scheduled an appointment with a counselor to figure out how to adapt to this new environment. I should have gotten a second opinion from the Wonderful Counselor, but I sunk deeper into depression.

My grades were slipping and I just couldn't grasp the information I was being taught. I studied as hard as I could and I only got "Cs" and "Ds."

I wanted to drop out of school and find a job, but before I made the decision to withdraw, I consulted the guidance counselor in my family, my uncle who used to work with college students in these situations.

He instructed me to take additional notes to accompany my class notes, and from there, to create note cards on key ideas and events and take them everywhere I went. He also got to the source of my sleepless nights and gruesome days. He asked how much balance I had. I told him I didn't have any and he also said that God was not going to fix the situation. He said that I must rearrange some things in my life.

It took a while, but I quickly learned to praise everywhere I went. I was tired of the enemy controlling my mind and body and making me think I was less of an individual because of the failures and setbacks that I endured. The enemy really made me believe that God had turned His back on me by my lack of commitment and focus on Him, but it really was my faith. I soon learned that giving thanks in times of spiritual drought will bring showers of peace.

The end of the semester was coming to a close. I fought hard, attended study groups, stayed in the library for hours, sought the Lord, fasted, read Scripture and filled my mind with positive promises from God's Word. Soon, all of the final exams were complete, the teacher evaluations were in, and the projects and portfolios were done. It was time for my grades to come in, and one week before I was to receive them, the Lord said that I was getting two sets of results. One result for my performance in school was given to me by computer and the other result for my act of praise was given by the master of design. He told me my first semester was a test to see if I would trust in Him or my intellect to get me through. He wanted to see if I would put confidence in my praise or my educational resources. He also knew that getting my degree was the most important thing at the time. That was my first mistake.

When I received my scholarship from the College of Journalism, I slowly allowed school to become my god, ahead of church, ministry and family. That's when I began to get depressed, the Lord told me. It was not that I couldn't adapt, it was all because I failed to realize God's first commandment of having no other gods before Him.

My classes and getting good grades literally became my drive and motivation, not pleasing the Lord with my whole heart. I started to skip services with excuses like, *"I have a test tomorrow, so I can't make it to service tonight pastor, I'll see you the next time."* My worship and gospel CD's started to collect dust and my Bibles were nowhere in sight.

Almighty Jehovah was blaming me for my downfall. *"I couldn't believe it,"* I said. *"You are the one who created me and guided me this far,"* I screamed. *"Why would You, the Great I Am, allow this to happen to me your servant, your child?"* He then put me in check. *When was the last time you got in my face and you didn't want anything from me, but wanting to give of yourself,* he asked? I knew exactly what He meant and it felt like an arrow had pierced my heart. While in high school, the Lord had me in intercession for my senior class for 3 months. I took my yearbook and prayed over every single picture in my class for God to enrich their lives upon graduation. Soon afterwards, I saw students seeking spiritual guidance from teachers who knew Christ, people were getting saved and weekly prayer meetings were established during the lunch periods with the Christian club.

He said that what caused me to slip back into depression was that I consulted everyone but Him when things got really tough. He added that, *"your prayers used to mean something, but when I began to test you, you stopped praying and you have the nerve to blame me for bringing back the fear and anxiety?"* I responded with an angry *"YES!"* I slowly stopped taking the pills the doctors prescribed and allowed the Lord to heal the pain.

Any individual who has suffered from or experienced suicidal thoughts and tendencies knows what it means to feel rejected. Rejection is one of the main factors causing someone to want to intentionally end their life. This includes feeling alone, out of place, uncomfortable like they are the only person in the world dealing with problems of failure, ridicule, being ignored or overlooked, not being accepted, the list is endless.

Back in the day, the saints of the church were taught, better yet, drilled on how to fear the Lord and walk in complete, total obedience to His word and every command. Some of them were literally scared straight to the altar in submission to accept the sacrifice offered from Christ Jesus. Those young folk growing up in the "old church" knew not to disobey the man or woman of God which included elders, parents, grandparents, aunts, uncles, mothers, deacons, pastors and all those in relation to them. The revelation of Hell's fire and brimstone not only came from the pulpit, but also could come from one forceful smack to the head if caught acting up in church or elsewhere. In those days, just one generation before mine, they actually lived a holy life, were saved and on average, were filled with the Spirit by their early teens or twenties. They enjoyed life. Why? It's because they pursued God fervently and wanted to make a change for the better.

A good friend of mine said in one of his sermons that, "change is not change until change is made." This is powerful.

That's the reason why our young people aren't stampeding the altar in repentance and are not seeking salvation. They don't want to change.

Does it really matter if I knew tarry personally (meaning an old ritual of tarrying at an altar in hopes of receiving the indwelling of the Holy Ghost,) or if I was filled by the laying on of hands? Acceptance from all people no matter what age is very important to a young person growing up in a world that does not know or understand them emotionally, physically or spiritually.

The reasoning behind the constant questioning and skepticism from the older saints to the younger ones in validation of their salvation is the gap of spiritual contentment. The inner man of these two generations have decades between them that foster unrest and misunderstandings for the lack of fellowship and communication. We must worship God TOGETHER without concerning ourselves with what songs should be sung (whether contemporary or traditional,) or with how Mother Daisy or Brother Stan is dressed, or who should pray the opening prayer. Frankly, WHO CARES! God doesn't even care about programs or outlined church services anyway, so why should you? Yes, He demands order and instructs total respect and reverence for His house, but it is more important that we just do what we were created to do—worship Him in His beauty and splendor.

The pressure to conform to the doctrine of the church and trying to fit into the mold set by my family was and still is difficult to fill. Again, being related to a preacher has its own responsibilities and struggles of being in the limelight of always being propped on a pedestal in the forefront. I felt an obligation to my family and to myself to set the standard before those under me as a humble servant to my shepherd and the ministry that God gave to my grandparents, but sometimes it does bring weariness.

There were many activities I wanted to do to enhance the youth ministry. I wanted "the body" to move from traditionalism to what was acceptable and new for the times. Under the backbone of strength and durability felt from my leaders, I folded and became defeated with the constant denial of my ideas. My intentions were prolonged until one afternoon in prayer when God spoke to me and said "Go Forth!"

I was so excited that I ran to my pastor's house yelling "Go forth, go forth!" Thankfully, my proposal was accepted and I was now able to express my love for God with my peers and friends who stood in agreement with me. I pray for all who are over a ministry or a specific department to have this feeling of freedom and belonging, and to learn to praise God in all that He has given you to do.

In times of distress, I'll praise you. When my life is a mess, I'll praise you. Just because you're God, I'll praise you. In my house, on my job, I'll praise you. As the storm clouds are brewing rain, I'll praise you. Down and out in my pain, I'll praise you. Ministering in dance, I'll praise you. The Kingdom will be my rightful stance and I'll praise you. Walking in love as a reflection of your light, I'll praise you. As I travel in blind faith, you guide me with your sight, and I'll still praise you.

CHAPTER 7

Accidents Happen

"And the Lord spake unto Moses and Aaron, Because ye believed me not, to sanctify me in the eyes of the children of Israel, therefore ye shall not bring this congregation into the land which I have given them." (Numbers 20:12 KJV)

It is better to obey than to sacrifice. Every time I did something wrong or was disobedient, this was what was said. I'm sad to say that I was and still am a little disobedient at times, but repentance is always an option. The key is to seek forgiveness and not fall prey to the enemy's trap that he has purposely set for us as children of God. But time and again, we fall back into our hidden habits and secret sins.

Moses was leader of the unappreciative, ungrateful Children of Israel who would have rather died in Egypt under Pharaoh's clutches than to be in the dry, flat and unfruitful wilderness. God knew what He was doing when He delivered them, but oh how quickly did they blame Him for their lack and starvation.

What puzzles me about the whole situation is their unwillingness to thank God for releasing them from the hand of the enemy and for providing their needs. Instead of complaining of not having any water or food, Moses

and Aaron did the only logical thing that could be done, to enter into the passion (presence) of the Lord.

Worship will bring glory and answers, but the instructions God gave to these men were crucial to them seeing the Promised Land flowing with milk and honey. Likewise, the Lord promised me some things, one of them being this book. In ministry, I have learned that sometimes you have to give more of yourself and put on hold what you would like to achieve for the benefit of others. No, I am not a pastor or a leader of a thriving congregation, but I am a part of several facets of leadership in the organization that I belong to, and that gives me the responsibility to be sensitive in my actions in the body of true believers. Partial obedience is disobedience, my grandmother would often say, and it is common to many. That is why we must not only know and study the Word of God; we must believe and be obedient to it.

After Moses was discovered by Pharoah's wife as a young baby, he grew up as a royal heir to the throne of his father.

All the while, his family and friends back home were slaves. How was he going to set them free and declare the promise of God in letting His people go? Well, let's fast forward 40 or so years; and now we are headed to the mountain top to receive the 10 most important rules on two slabs of stone. After Moses received the commandments from the Lord, he witnessed his people worshipping idol gods and bowing to a golden calf. He, I'm sure, was devastated and disappointed, but the Lord knew that soon His people were to be free once again.

In the meantime, Moses was given directions from God to speak to the rock and the water would follow. For some unknown reason, Moses gathered the assembly around the rock, but he smote it instead of speaking to it, not only once, but twice out of frustration. Although his actions did in fact get the desired result, but the means to getting the water was NOT what God wanted, and therefore the Children of Israel suffered by not having their leader enter into the promise land with them. Shortcuts to our blessings are not always guaranteed. We know what God wants us to do, but when we go against His word in any way, God will reward, but not without consequences.

My lesson about being obedient in all things came in an unusual way. The gateway to freedom outside my home was the comfort of the car my mother gave to me. Her 2000 Honda Civic was just the right size and color, but most of the time I would only go to church, stores and then back home. Sometimes I would call and inform them of where I was going and at other times, I wouldn't. Not because I was out to do something unholy, but I honestly felt if I was going to church instead of going home from work, then that should be my decision without any input from my parents. I mean glorifying God in the fellowship of other believers is more important than being home wasting idle time, right?

On one summer afternoon, I was surfing the Internet and checking my e-mail on one of my many accounts when my profile indicated I had a new message. I didn't know who the sender was, but I guessed a male by the way the address was written. There was no title in the subject box either, and I was a little reluctant to read it, but I opened it anyway. It read: *"...There are at least 3 specific miracles about to happen for you, the Lord is about to drop a book in your spirit, concerning the life of a woman of God. Next, the Lord is placing KEYS in your hands concerning access spiritually and naturally, and the last thing is, the Lord is about to OPEN UP THE BUSINESS IN YOU, for He calls you an ADMINISTRATOR and you shall be the BACK BONE of the ministry saith the Lord... In turn, all of this will create so much favor in your life even concerning SCHOOL! For the spirit of a DOCTOR is on you to care for His people mentally and physically."*

The very next evening was a Thursday and after I returned home from Bible Study, I received a call from one of my best friends. She told me that she was in Bible Study when the Lord spoke to her concerning a receptionist for her Christian dance studio. Her former employee was not saved and she was having some problems with that individual spiritually and professionally, so she wanted to know if I was available to aid her in her business for the glory of God. She wanted someone who was saved, had a bubbly personality and worked well with parents and children. I told her that I would pray about it and get back with her. As soon as I got off the phone, the Lord said, "Yes." We scheduled a date of when I was going to start work and a few weeks later, I met the parents of the children who were planning to enroll in the dance classes. I informed her of the prophecy that the apostle said to me and she said the word was for her. We both prayed before the first class confirming that the Spirit of the Lord would orchestrate every avenue of her business and ministry to offer children and adults a Christian atmosphere where expressions of dance and creative movement are sought and felt in each practice and performance.

After about two weeks of answering phones and managing a database, I was returning home from class when I decided to go to church for prayer meeting. Earlier that afternoon, I told my parents that after I got off from work, I was going home to rest, but I wanted to go to church instead. I pulled out of the parking lot and within half a mile I was in the left turning lane of a major intersection about to turn onto the street where my church was located. It was Tuesday exactly one week and four days before I was to graduate from the University of Florida. It was approximately 7:30 pm in the evening. The light turned green, and I slowly drove up to the traffic light following the cars in front of me thinking traffic was clear for the turn. All of a sudden, I heard a car horn blowing at me and I didn't stop. I froze. I was traveling about 12 miles an hour and the other vehicle between 35 and 50 miles/hour. The driver slammed into my passenger front door and caused my car to spin in the opposite direction. The air bags deployed, the windshield was shattered and my glasses flew from my face onto the floor in the back right-hand side of the car. Shock overwhelmed me, but one of my good friends from church saw the accident and comforted me while she called my father who was already at church.

Unfortunately, I was at fault and got my first traffic ticket. I was burned on my right arm from the air bag and my left knee had a large bruise. The seatbelt caused a small bruise to form on the left side of my neck just under my left ear and the inside of my check was lacerated from the whiplash and the impact of the accident. Once again, God proved Himself strong and protected me and I was able to walk away from the accident with only minor scars and bruises.

My mother met me at the scene and helped me talk to police and firemen about what happened. She then met my father at the hospital. Three hours passed before I ever saw a physician and no one examined me except the nurse. I tried to explain to my parents that I was fine, but they insisted that I get checked out. All the while, my thoughts of the day ran across my mind. That lesson taught me how important it is to be obedient in all things, no matter how trivial the circumstance may seem.

For those who are reading this and have yet to be obedient to His commands, large or small, I beg you to evaluate your life in terms of relationships, occupations, your way of living and your journey with the Father.

You might find yourself spending hours at a time working to filter out what is and what's not in line with God's word, but it will be worth it once you finally free yourself of what's been hindering you from God's plan for your life. The day will come when all will have to stand before the Lord and give account of everything we have done here on earth.

Just make sure before that day approaches, your purpose and motivation is to strive to do all you can to honor the Lord in your service to others and your neighbors. Discard the things that are keeping you from accepting and carrying out whatever the Lord has commissioned you to do. I pray that you find your true identity and hopefully you will not ignore who God has called you to be in His kingdom.

CHAPTER 8

A New Beginning

Therefore if any man be in Christ, he is a new creature: old things are passed away; behold, all things are become new. (2 Corinthians 5:17 KJV)

His grace is sufficient. His love is everlasting. His power is immeasurable. His peace surpasses all understanding. His blood covers all. His character is unchangeable. His glory is revealing. His promise is sure. His life is matchless. His word is enough. His reign is righteous. His yoke is easy, and His burden is light.

Webster defines grace as God's unmerited love for man, but I know His grace to be so much more. Words don't seem adequate to describe His love for us, but I would like to think His death, burial and resurrection are enough for me. His life brings curiosity, controversy and popularity in religious commentary and theology. His credentials far exceed any scholastic endeavor and His miracles are too many to count. Amazingly, His love is experienced every day with the rising of the sun each morning.

From my birth, to the fire, and the car accident, God's grace has been following me since my debut on earth. What if I did not accept the Lord in the pardon of my sins, would His grace still rain on me in my sinful life?

Would He still shower His mercy on men and women who do not live for Him? No matter what our spiritual condition, God's grace is the same for all and He bore the cross for everyone. As we pray for our enemies and those who persecute us, as it states in Matthew 5:44-45, God will, *"give his sunlight to both the evil and the good, and [will send] rain on the just and the unjust alike." (NLT)*

His grace saves us, secures us and sanctifies us. His saving grace is the voluntary generosity and provision of salvation that is free to all who believe and call on his name. At Calvary on Golgotha's Hill, God's divine intervention proved His majestic power when the people thought it was the end. He declared, "It is finished." He was right. The sins of mankind were finished by the blood that was seen dripping on the wooden cross, but little did the Roman soldiers know that those words were the cue to something bigger and more spectacular that awaited them just 3 more days when He rose from the borrowed tomb.

In spite of our sins and our wayward actions, God's grace keeps and seals our relationship with Him. It is our faith in Him that brings grace. *"Therefore, since we have been made right in God's sight by faith, we have peace with God because of what Jesus Christ our Lord has done for us. Because of our faith, Christ has brought us into this place of undeserved privilege where we now stand, and we confidently and joyfully look forward to sharing God's glory." (Romans 5:1-2 NLT)*

Grace is solely based on the Lord's work and is undeserved by man. Due to our sinful nature, we are not entitled to His free gift, but the Holy Spirit grants us the freedom to experience the fruit of His abundant love. *"And since it is through God's kindness, then it is not by their good works. For in that case, God's grace would not be what it really is-free and undeserved." (Romans 11:6 NLT)*

If we had the chance to supply our own salvation, the cost would be too great, but God's demonstration of Grace to the world was His Son Jesus Christ.

By God's sacrificial act of freely giving His son as a ransom for our sins, we are redeemed and have right standing with the Father. *"Being justified freely by his grace through the redemption that is in Christ Jesus..." (Romans 3:24 KJV)* The greatest truth of our redemption is that grace is free without any pre-existing qualifications or actions on our part. Even those who are unworthy have the opportunity to experience

His presence because Christ loves everyone the same. We are all His favorites.

Through His grace and love for us, He in turn wants us to be strong in what we have learned by relying on His power and strength. An example of this thought is in II Timothy chapter 2, verses 1 and 2 where Paul encourages Timothy to be strong in the grace of Jesus by teaching others of His blessings and favor. *"Thou therefore, my son, be strong in the grace that is in Christ Jesus. And the things that thou hast heard of me among many witnesses, the same commit thou to faithful men, who shall be able to teach others also."*

When Jesus began his ministry, he did not train twelve men to only recruit hundreds of thousands to the Lord in Jerusalem, Judea and Samaria. A worldwide revolution is growing with individuals who want to learn how to partake of His glory. We all want the atmosphere and the elegance of heaven to be released in the earth. It's even mentioned when we pray, *"Thy kingdom come. Thy will be done, in earth as it is in heaven." (Matthew 6:10 KJV)*

In our yearning for this glorious ambiance, remember to keep ministry first. God wants His children to be happy and successful in life, but His ultimate goal for this world is to be saved. The very world that rejected Him, He wants to forgive and mend the relationship between His creation (mankind) and God (the Father of grace).

So, I ask you to accept His free offer of salvation and invite His Spirit to control your life. As you begin to follow Him, you will be tested, tried and shaken. This will happen only to test your faith and your trust in the Father. Walk in the gifts of grace and love that only God can give as you develop and continue your spiritual journey.

CHAPTER 9

On a Quest for Love

"Now may the God of peace make you holy in every way, and may your whole spirit and soul and body be kept blameless until our Lord Jesus Christ comes again." (1 Thessalonians 5:23 NLT)

After I received my undergraduate degree from the University of Florida, I thought the sky was the limit and anything was possible. Boy was I in for a rude awakening. Journalism is hard, I mean extremely hard. In terms of gathering necessary information, interviewing subjects, actually going to the site of the action and just trying to simplify what you want to say is daunting. The market for journalists in newspaper or feature writing in my town was scarce. Yes, we had several outlets where I could have been a full time staff member, but my aspirations were changing.

At the age of 24, I was heavily involved in ministry at my church and was content being single. One day while looking for employment online, a friend of mine suggested I look into building a relationship with a young man named Alonzo Lucas. To say the least, I was a little hesitant, but I did receive a phone call from him and the rest was history. We officially met in July of 2007 in Jacksonville, Florida at a church convention. I found out later that he lived in Sumter, South Carolina and he moved to Baldwin, Florida to follow his high school sweetheart. His journey to find love was quite interesting, but we will discover the full details a little later. He is the youngest son of 8 siblings and has 4 sisters and 3 brothers.

I don't know if it was love at first sight, but he seemed to have a place in my heart. Upon our meeting, my brother told my mother "For some reason, I believe this Mr. Lucas is going to be my brother-in-law." These were his exact words. Of course, I was surprised and embarrassed at the statement, but maybe God did have something up His sleeve. My first official date with Alonzo was at Bally Hoo's restaurant. We invited several friends along to celebrate me and another friend's birthday. I could hardly enjoy my meal because I was so nervous and excited. My friends were curious as to why I was staring at this young man so hard, but I'm sure they knew the process of young love was beginning.

First Thessalonians 5:23 states when courting someone, we should be attracted to the other person physically, emotionally and intellectually (spiritually). If a person does not meet all the criteria, then you are wasting your time if you are planning to have a Godly relationship. God's purpose is to have both parties consecrate themselves to prepare their bodies, souls and spirits for a long, fulfilling relationship that involves a constant renewal to be committed and whole before the Him. "May God himself, the God who makes everything holy and whole, make you holy and whole, put you together—spirit , soul, and body—and keep you fit for the coming of our Master, Jesus Christ. The one who called you is completely dependable. If he said it, he'll do it!" (1 Thessalonians 5:23-24, MSG)

In terms of a job, I finally began working at a local law firm assisting with various administrative duties, but on October 22, 2007, my prayers were answered when I became employed as the Court Information Receptionist at the local Criminal Courthouse. The position allowed me to meet a variety of people from all walks of life. Some had dire situations as extreme as killing someone to lesser offenses such as drug possession or traffic violations.

My greatest satisfaction came when I was able to tell others about Jesus. It was very rewarding to share the gospel because in sensitive situations, it's comforting to know there is hope in the Lord. No matter what the judge may say, God is still in control. As I was coming back from lunch one afternoon, I found several post-it notes near my computer station with prayer requests ranging from sickness and deliverance to receiving good grades. My response was, "OK, God, I guess I must be doing something right." Half of the notes were from people I knew, and I was reluctant to begin interceding for them because I knew the sacrifice it took to constantly commission God on the behalf of others.

By this time, Alonzo and I were establishing a strong relationship and for some reason I began to feel that he might in fact be "the one," but I didn't want to rush into that mode just yet. After about 6 months, the Lord began to deal with us concerning our future as a couple as possible life partners. During this time of consecration, we both wrote a list of things we wanted the Lord to do for our lives. We constantly prayed and fasted collectively and individually during the Spring of 2008 because we knew marriage was soon to come.

Now it is time to learn how Alonzo got to Florida in the first place. The following paragraphs are Mr. Lucas' personal account concerning his quest for love. Get your tissue out because the tears are going to fall.

The Move

In the winter of 2005, I was blessed to [receive] my Master of Arts degree while living in Sumter, South Carolina. At the time, I was engaged to my high school sweetheart, (we will refer to her as Ms. T), and never really conceptualized moving to another state. My family of origin lived in South Carolina so this is where I was most comfortable; however, love will often take an individual out of his/her comfort zone. By the time I completed my Master's program, Ms. T had been in Gainesville, Florida for several years pursuing her educational and career goals. Since there was close to a six hour distance between Sumter and Gainesville, I often became love sick. I wanted us to marry and live in Sumter, but God had other plans.

Ms. T was studying to receive her J.D. degree at the University of Florida. With certain laws varying from state to state, she would have to practice law in Florida. One option for me was to have a long distance marriage. This would mean we would commute on the weekends, then depart for the work week. Another option would have me move to Gainesville. I chose the latter. Prior to moving knew I needed to secure employment in or around Alachua County. Due to the distance, I was [given] the opportunity to complete several phone interviews. In December of 2005, I was offered a position in Macclenny, Florida that was to start in January of 2006. Macclenny was about an hour from Gainesville, so the commute was not that bad.

Even though I moved to Florida as a means of getting closer to Ms. T, it seemed as if we were growing further apart. In 2006, I began feeling God's prompting towards the call of [the] ministry. During that time, I was led to spend a lot of time in fasting and prayer. During one of my prayer times, approximately six months after moving to Florida, I heard the voice of the Lord telling me to [cease] all lines of communication with Ms. T until further notice. Honestly, I recall feeling confused about the instructions; however, I was obedient. When I told Ms. T, she also seemed confused, but who are we to question God?

This was my first time living alone in 26 years. Mind you, I come from a large family who all resided under the same roof, and because of that, I was not able to have the intimacy with God like I did in 2006. For one month, I did not call or visit Ms. T., and fasted as God instructed. At the end of the month, I called Ms. T., as I felt released to do so. During this time, she assumed that I had broken up with her. Over the course of our 11-12 year courtship, we broke up and got back together several times; however, she felt that me not calling or seeing her was too much. We both agreed to go our separate ways. As a result of the break up, I was extremely hurt and more confused than ever. I moved to an unknown place (away from family and friends) to be closer to her, but this [move] allowed me to be closer to God.

Shortly afterwards, I confided in my pastor for Godly counsel. My pastor reassured me through the scripture in John 15: 1-7. He used this spiritual analogy to explain why we broke up. He noted that there are people who are connected to us which hinder our growth. As a result, God breaks those connections so we can become closer to Him. Although this made me feel some better, I still felt a void in my life. I was closer to God, but at the same time, I had a desire to be married. In 2007, I went on several dates with different women; however, I was not comfortable in developing a long term union with any of them. Truth be told, I was torn and broken because it was difficult to open my heart to love another person.

Later that summer, I received a call from a church friend named Robert. During this call, he stated that his friend Jessica was looking to start a Christian step team. I basically said thanks, but no thanks. I didn't know how to dance much less step for that matter. A day or two passed and I received another call from him. During our conversation, he told Jessica that I was not interested in participating in the step team, but she wanted me to call her anyway. He gave me .her number and I called. Due to personal reservations, I blocked my phone number. I called and introduced myself and told Jessica what I told Robert. She informed me that she told Robert that she was fine with my decision.

At that time, I realized Robert tricked me into connecting with Jessica. Over the course of the next few weeks, we talked for hours as if we had known each other for years. In our discussions, we quickly learned we had a lot in common. We both were heavily involved in ministry, had a sense of humor and we were single. It seemed as if the brokenness and distrust disappeared as I grew to know her. I also found out that she ironically was the niece of Pastor M. Look at God. The same person He used to comfort me in my despair would someday be my uncle, Wow God!!! This added new meaning to Romans 8:28. "And we know that all things work together for the good of them that love God, to them who are the called according to his purpose."

Now, wasn't that just a lovely story? Our steps are surely ordered by the Lord because I never knew my first relationship would turn into a fulfilling one. Moving on to about a year later in the summer of 2008, my birthday was around the corner and Monday, July 7th was truly one I will always cherish. After I got to my parent's home from work, I received a call from Alonzo asking if I had some free time because he was on the way to see me. I said "Yes," and a little after 6:00 that evening, I opened the door and the next few moments literally changed my life.

As I sat on the couch next to my mother, he took my hand and reminisced about our meeting and how he felt God was leading him to pursue a wife. All the while, I was thinking this is the day that every little girl dreams of, but I was so nervous about why he was talking like this. By this time, he was on one knee and pulled out a small brown teddy bear with a red bow tie. Behind the Velcro enclosure was a box, that I thought held a pair of earrings. I'm glad I was wrong because it was an engagement ring. He then asked, "How would you feel if we spent the rest of our lives together?" I was silent as I turned to look at my mother in disbelief as I was trying to fathom what just happened. After about 10 seconds, I screamed and said "Yes, I would love to spend the rest of my life with you." After my extraordinary early birthday gift, I ran outside to where my father and uncle were working and screamed in excitement flashing the ring. My father's response was priceless. "I give you my blessing, but you all need to hurry up and do what you need to do before I change my mind." Way to go, Dad. He is definitely a character in every way.

In the back of my mind, I knew this day would come, not this soon, but I was happy Alonzo saw fit to choose me to be his bride. The evening continued with hugs and congratulations from a family member and a friend who witnessed the proposal stating. "Today is a special day for the Phillips family." I replied "Yes, it is, it surely is a special day."

As we attended our monthly meeting with the church, there was an evident glow on my face. One of the elders wanted to know why I was so happy. I then showed him my new gift, and he said "Well, praise the Lord." I said, "The Lord is good," just to show a little humor. Our prayers were being answered and we were thankful for where He was planning to lead us as a couple.

In the coming weeks, the wedding plans were underway. I already had our wedding coordinator in mind. She was a young lady who was an event coordinator with the extraordinary HolyLand Experience in Orlando, Florida. In one of our meetings, she said that I was one of the most organized and efficient brides-to-be that she has ever worked with. Basically within 4 months, most of the ground work was already complete with us contacting and securing the wedding party, the caterer, the decorator, the officiating minister, the photographer and videographer and the like because I wanted my wedding day to be perfect. All Alonzo had to do was show up at the altar in his white suit, anxiously waiting for me to walk down the aisle.

August 1, 2009 was the date we chose. We wanted it to be a free Saturday where the Florida Gator football team had an away game. My family are Gator fans, so we didn't want any excuses for those who could not attend because of the game. Yes, I was a little selfish, but I thought, this was the most important day of my life, and I wanted it to be all about me. Our engagement lasted for exactly one year and 25 days, yes, to some, that may seem a little long, but I wanted to be double sure we were ready to become one.

During the time of preparation, we sought the Lord daily and received counsel from our pastor on several occasions who provided spiritual and practical lessons and guidelines for us to follow. Since both of our families were in the ministry, we had several good examples of couples who were at one time in our shoes. My parents, at the time had been married for 31 years and Alonzo's parents had been together for a little over 40 years. Now with numbers like those, we knew with God, any and all things are possible.

After months of planning, the big day finally came on Saturday, August 1, 2009. Family, friends and loved ones were anxiously awaiting for the church doors to open as my father proudly walked me down the aisle. As I entered the sanctuary, my eyes were instantly fixed on my husband who was already trying to hold back tears. In the background, "A Whole New World," was being sung and as the ceremony continued, the moment came for my father to give me, his only daughter away. I could only imagine what was going through his mind as he prepared to make his statement. What he said next was truly hilarious. When the minister said 'Who is the one that gives away this bride?" Mr. Phillips replied "Her mother and myself" and gestured to the congregation that he had his eyes on Alonzo. The sanctuary erupted in laughter. I just wanted him to act right this one day, but at least he didn't embarrass me too bad. Looking back on my wedding day, I must say it was special and I would do it all over again. To know that you are joined together with the person God intended for you to be with is amazing, and after 11 years of marriage, we do believe His plan for our lives will be great.

CHAPTER 10

Learning to Trust in Him

"For even though I am absent from you in body, nevertheless I am with you in spirit. [I am] delighted to see your good discipline...and to see the stability of your faith in Christ, your steadfast reliance on Him and your unwavering confidence in His power, wisdom and goodness."
(Colossians 2:5, AMP)

The honeymoon in Nassau, Bahamas was over and now it was time for reality to set in. We were officially declared a married couple, and with all of the responsibility of keeping a home, maintaining the finances and just working together as a team, was established on Monday, August 10, 2009. Up until this point, all of the bills were taken care of. I never had the chance to live on my own, not by choice, but I went from my parent's home to my own. Our first year was wonderful. We purchased a brand new home, which we financed up front without a loan, a new car was purchased with only 9 miles, and our first child was on the way. We were ecstatic that in 9 months, we were going to be parents. In all of the excitement with our family, there was one situation that truly rocked me to the core. In March of 2011, my mother contracted breast cancer.

Thousands of questions were going through my head as to why God would allow this to happen. After mom told us the news, I remember responding by saying, "Well, that's unfortunate to hear, but you and dad are going to be grandparents later this year and I need your help with this new little one." My mother's attitude completely changed. She knew she had something to live and fight for, despite what the doctors were saying.

In March 2017 I sat my mom down for a short interview on her reaction when she discovered she had breast cancer. She shared her thoughts and feelings.

> "1. What was your initial reaction to receiving the news of you having breast cancer?
>
> 'I was shocked and devastated.'

2. Did you notice any symptoms?

   'I did not. I went for my regular mammogram, which is where it was detected.'

3. Did you [do] any preventative [tasks] to decrease your chances?

   'No, because I never expected to have cancer. I made sure that I had my annual mammogram. Cancer did not run in either side of my family. I cried when I felt like it.'

4. Did you question God? Was your faith in Him unsteady at any time?

   'I did have a moment of 'Why me, Lord?', but I quickly realized that with God, I could make it. I told my doctor, when I first got the news, that 'I shall live, and not die!'

5. How did you encourage yourself when times were difficult and painful?

   'I wrote in my journal every day. I read the Bible a lot. I also read books and magazines regarding breast cancer survivors. I cried when I felt like it.

6. How did your family and friends respond to the news?

    'They were surprised, but very supportive. I never felt alone. My husband was right by my side. I received phone calls every day for months.'

I am proud and thankful to say my mother is cancer free and is a testament to God's awesome healing power. While mom was battling breast cancer, my husband and I were preparing to groom another life. During my first few months, all I could think about was whether I was going to have a miscarriage. As mentioned in Chapter 1, my mother had 5 miscarriages prior to me entering the world, so I had hoped this would not be my story.

Thankfully, Miss Madison Bijan Lucas was born on Sunday, November 20, 2011 at 5:18 p.m. weighing 8 pounds and 4 ounces. Yes, the young lady who was born premature at 1 pound, 4 ounces grew up and had a huge gift. After being in labor for over 8 hours, Madison arrived looking blue with the umbilical cord wrapped around her neck screaming to the top of her lungs. Of course, she was struggling to breathe, but within a few minutes, her pigment was normal. After my husband and I cried for a few moments, what happened next was truly a miracle. One of the doctors handed me a jar with what looked like a section of someone's intestine. She told me the substance was an enormous cyst about the size of a small grapefruit. It had been growing on my uterus and if it would have burst, we would have lost the baby. To God be the glory!!!!!

Four days before Madison's first birthday, my season came to an end at the Alachua County Criminal Justice Center. During my 5 years with Court Administration, my family endured several tests and trials all to prove God's mighty power. One of them was sickness. My husband has several health issues, from depression and anxiety to heart problems, just to name a few. There were several occasions where he would tell me he was in the emergency room for chest pain and he would be released within a few days. This was ongoing since we met in 2007, and now 5 years later, the medical bills were piling up. We were slowly accumulating a lot of debt and keeping up with our household expenses were proving to be quite overwhelming.

I had my bouts with depression and have suffered from multiple anxiety attacks, all triggered from stress and worry. In those moments, I would find solace from God's Word and by singing hymns. One of the scriptures I used to comfort me was Isaiah 41:10 "Don't be afraid for I am with you. Don't be discouraged, for I am your God. I will strengthen you and help you. I will hold you up with my victorious right hand." The Lord promises to cover and protect us during difficult times, but even in the encouragement we were receiving, I still doubted God. My faith at the time was not solid due to our current situation. All the while, I looked to my husband to fix everything when I should have been trusting God to meet our needs.

The financial strain continued, and while receiving unemployment, I still managed to remain hopeful trusting God would bless me with another job. Learning to trust in the Lord was evident every month when bills were due. There were several nights I cried asking God how we were going to make it, but my husband reassured me every time that, "It won't be like this always, and God will see us through." After almost 7 months of not having a job, I was blessed to be employed as a member of the state of Florida under the Agency for Persons with Disabilities.

Working with disabled men and women on a daily basis was a culture shock. I had to deal with individuals who were not able to talk, walk or feed themselves. It made me realize how thankful I am to be able to do things on my own, without assistance from another, and it taught the value of humility and servanthood. In order for us to fully understand and walk in obedience to God, we must submit ourselves as servants to those who are downtrodden and destitute. How then can we say we love God, if we don't love, care for and respect our brothers and sisters?

When I was 12 or 13 years old, my grandfather spoke into my life declaring I was to be a missionary. Of course, I blew it off because the notion of me evangelizing and being hospitable to others was NOT on my radar at all. He was right. In July of 2010, at 27 years of age, I was consecrated as a missionary with the Church of God by Faith all thanks to one small seed from a wise man. I say all of that to say this, never underestimate your ability when it comes to venturing out in new territory. God can take you places if you are obedient and have a willing spirit. So to Bishop Emeritus James McKnight, thanks for trusting me to carry the mantle.

The Lord has been with me since day one teaching me through the good, bad and utterly gruesome times, He has shown His glory. The very breath we breathe is all because of His grace. Being able to drive a vehicle, to move and be active is all because of God. Even when our faith is small or uncertain, He still proves Himself strong.

One morning as I retrieved the mail, I noticed an envelope from the Eighth Judicial Circuit Court. Instantly, my heart sank because I knew what the information inside was about. Prior to this particular notice, we were several months behind on our mortgage, and contacted our mortgager to make arrangements. The stress of keeping our home had gotten to be too much for us as we had other household bills. I got into the car and drove home crying because I did not want to tell my husband that it was a foreclosure notice.

Yes, we were in the process of losing our home. The home we had shared so many memories in was about to be taken away.

After telling my husband about the notice, he had such a peace that it totally caught me off guard. I was hysterical, upset and disappointed. The thought of us starting over again was definitely devastating, but when I looked into his eyes, I knew we were going to be fine. During the process of looking into other homes, the desire to settle in and begin another set of memories was our focus, and the last day in our home was bittersweet. I still think on this day often as we packed up our vehicles and the UHAUL truck with boxes of mementos and furniture. Our neighbors were saddened of our loss, but hopeful and optimistic in our next move. The home we were moving into was fully furnished and did need a lot of improvements, but thanks to family and some skillful hands in the community, we made it through the process and in February of 2015, had our first day as a family in the home.

In every instance in my life from losing my job and dealing with depression to the loss of our home, I had to learn to fully trust and depend on God to carry my family in those trying times. It was a rough road to travel, and there were many times I wanted to give up, but God reassured me He would always be there at every happy, sad and dark moment giving instructions on where and what to do. I am also thankful for those who encouraged me and my family through prayer, words of wisdom and Scripture. We are grateful that you had a hand in teaching us how to trust in Him.

It reminds me of Job. Job 29:11-16 give a great example of what it means to be a servant for those in need.

> *"All who heard me praised me. All who saw me spoke well of me. For I assisted the poor in their need and the orphans who required help. I helped those without hope, and they blessed me...I caused the widows' hearts to sing for joy. Everything I did was honest. Righteousness covered me like a robe, and I wore justice like a turban. I served as eyes for the blind and feet for the lame. I was a father to the poor and assisted strangers who needed help" (Job 29: 11-16, NLT)*

Most of us are all familiar with Job's account, but in all he endured, he still found time to honor God. By telling of times past where the Lord blessed him to be an asset to his community, his spirit assured him that all would be well if he continued serving others. Speaking on those same lines, one of my favorite hymns is, "It is Well with My Soul," by Phillip P. Bliss (1838 -1876). The stanza "Though Satan should buffet, though trials should come, let this blest assurance control, that, Christ has regarded my helpless estate, and hath shed His own blood for my soul" literally transformed my thinking. Many times, I asked God when it would all end, but in this hymn, I found comfort knowing my lasting Provider would come to my rescue.

Yes, we all have had our share of tests and trials. They are essential on our Christian journeys, but in those difficult times, it is how we respond that moves the heart of God. During Job's most trying and darkest times, he still managed to have a heart of thanksgiving and gratitude. Those individuals whom he confided in thought the worst of him thinking he had sinned in some way, but Job understood his role as a servant to his God and to others through genuine compassion for the human spirit.

Just as Job spent his life in pursuit of helping others through the love of God, I, too, from a young age, had and still have a passion to give to my fellow man. While most kids were out at the mall with their friends or going to watch movies, my brother and I were visiting nursing homes and the sick. We would often sing inspirational hymns along with other missionary workers and give encouragement through Biblical applications and prayer. Man, what a way to spend an afternoon after 6 long hours of hard labor at school. I would dread Wednesday afternoons because between 3:00 and 4:00, I knew I had to focus on what the Lord had commissioned me to do. Thankfully, being from a Christian family, my parents and grandparents instilled in me the values of faithfulness, commitment, service and love for all people.

CHAPTER 11

Renewed Faith

"The faithful love of the Lord never ends! His mercies never cease. Great is his faithfulness; his mercies begin afresh each morning. I say to myself, 'The Lord is my inheritance; therefore, I will hope in Him!'" (Lamentations 3:22-24 NLT)

At this moment reflecting on the events that have transpired in my life, I can honestly say the Lord has been faithful and true at every stage. His promises for us are to experience new beginnings each day. As the scripture says, God's mercies, His grace and love are fresh and new every morning. This means when we are given the opportunity to witness another day, we should be thankful for being able to receive a fresh start.

My story is a testament of steadfast commitment and renewed faithfulness. From the moment I entered the world,

I had to fight to live, fight for my faith and my marriage. When I was born, the enemy knew my future and wanted to take me out before I realized my purpose. We as believers must acknowledge our worth and value as assets to the kingdom. Our very existence poses a threat to the kingdom of darkness, but as we receive more knowledge and truth about "why" we were created and to "whom" we belong, then we can take our rightful place as men and women of God.

It was around 10:30 pm on Saturday, September 15, 2007. As I was preparing for bed, my bedroom became extremely cold for some reason. An eerie presence entered the room as I fell into a deep sleep. I took a deep breath only to be interrupted by the angel of death. Frightened and confused, I began to go into dream land and found myself in a gym on a volleyball team. The opposing team, dressed in black and gray uniforms kept yelling "You shall be defeated, and this night, your life will end."

All the while as I was playing on my team, my teammates, dressed in white and powder blue uniforms were encouraging me with various scriptures and promises from God's Word. When it was my turn to serve, several rings of fire circled me and my team. The score at the time was 8 to 12 with the opposing team in the lead. Every time they scored, I was hit with a fiery dart causing me to stumble into the rings of fire. My entire body was burning, but I continued to play as I was not consumed by the deadly arrows.

Throughout the game, my teammates continued to declare God's Word and ensured my life was worth fighting for and that I was going to live. During the grueling match, their words finally started to resonate in my spirit and my team began to get the upper hand after about an hour of intense combat. I soon began to say the name of Jesus over and over again softly as sweat ran into my eyes. Now mind you, I was still asleep, but the dream I was having seemed so real that I actually started to sweat and my linen became wet with perspiration. From that experience, the Holy Spirit said "Not this one," and the angel of death left immediately allowing my team to win in the end. I knew I had to devote my entire life to the Lord from that point on because He obviously had something extraordinary for me in the coming years, and the journey to find the "extraordinary" thing was to be enjoyable.

What felt like several hours was about 45 minutes from the time I first fell asleep at 10:30 pm. Finally, after waking up, I felt heavy and drained like I just lost a boxing match. I surely am grateful for not losing the volleyball game because I believe the dream was symbolic of our daily lives as Christians learning to maneuver and strategize in our many battles with the adversary.

In some circumstances, my commitment to follow Christ actually caused my faith to remain sure despite opposition from various outlets. In retrospect, God truly gets the glory.

Even while battling anxiety, depression and the many pitfalls of growing up a young Christian woman, I stood strong and continued to give whenever I could. I suffered in silence for years trying to contemplate God's reasoning for all the turmoil and difficulty I endured. In the process of lamenting, which is the point between despair and hope, my father often reminded me that prayer is the weapon we need to win our battles. Of course, the power of prayer brings substantial, life-changing results, but it also takes a lot of work to petition the Lord. I found out soon enough that consistency is key to moving the heart of God.

In my younger days, prayer was second nature. Every morning at 5:00 am, I began my day praying and thanking Him for the little things like waking up, being able to see, you know the obvious things. Then, worship filled the space to where God's presence literally transformed the scene. After 30 minutes, I would get ready for work and my commute also consisted of prayer. I found myself communing with God several times throughout the day. Understand that a focused, determined young woman plus prayer, equals a force to be reckoned with.

As women, most of us naturally nurture, care and give our all to our families and communities. This instinct is power when directed to the right source. Our natural God-given ability to raise, love and mother our children goes beyond our homes, it reaches to other people as our greatest commandment from the Lord: To love others as he loved us (John 15:12). So it is with our prayer time. Whatever we are determined or driven to do, whether that may be to own a business, start writing a book or just be an overall better individual comes with us getting in line with His plan, and allowing prayer to direct all our endeavors.

As I became older, my prayers ceased. The relationship with my husband suffered as a result because I had to grow as a young wife in terms of allowing my husband to take his rightful place as the priest of our home. Anyone who knows me knows I am a take charge, direct person who is extremely strong willed. There were times where submission was and still is an issue. The Scripture where wives are supposed to submit to their husbands conflicts with my agenda. Personally, I believe spouses should have an equal share of leading in some way. I often ask myself, "Why can't husbands submit to wives at least 30 percent of the time?" God did give the responsibility of leading the home and providing for the family to men, but that's not always the case in terms of mothers raising kids on their own.

At any rate, my relationship suffered for a long time because we both were confused as to what our specific roles were. Yes, we knew on the surface the things we had to do, but spiritually and Biblically, we had no idea. That might seem weird coming from two people who grew up in Christian homes and went to church at least three times a week.

The reason for the difficulty in understanding our roles was because our prayers as a couple stopped. The communication and intimacy with God were few and far in-between. Many nights I cried myself to sleep trying to figure out why we had become so distant. I didn't understand the lack of prayer with our Savior was the start of our downfall.

It wasn't until after work one night, the Holy Spirit spoke and said, I was the one to bring my family back spiritually. I knew all along He was prompting me to get back on track with my prayer life, but I was so hurt by what had transpired, that I honestly did not feel like praying at all. I purposefully set my alarm to go off at 4:30 am to intercede on my family's behalf. Why at this ungodly hour, would I spend one hour with the Lord? Well, I'm glad you asked. I had to condition and discipline my spirit in terms of the warfare that was to come. I was not going to allow Satan to intrude on my family any longer. Basically, I had enough of his shenanigans, tricks and lies. The defeat I was feeling had to stop, and the only way for that to happen, was getting face down before the Lord.

In order for you to fully receive all that you are entitled to, you have to put in the work without any shortcuts. Yes, fasting is a requirement. Yes, making sacrifices are a requirement. Letting go of certain people and things you enjoyed are all requirements. I was willing to take the steps for my family to once again live in the peace that surpasses all understanding. Are you willing to make that choice?

In my decision to revamp my prayer life, the faith I had once lost in the Lord and in my husband became renewed and rejuvenated. In every aspect of our relationship from the way we raise our children, to managing the home, even to how we address each other was beginning to change for the better. It was all due to us inviting the Lord in to finally take control.

Allowing time to bask in God's Word and submit to His teachings were essential in us coming together. In a matter of months, our relationship completely turned around and the spark in both of our lives returned and caused us to love in a deeper, more fulfilling manner. What brought us together was prayer and prayer will continue to keep us.